Reconstruction:
Binding the Wounds

Edited by Cheryl Edwards

Cartoonist Tom Nast showed freed slaves heading West and the persecuted Chinese moving East in the 1870s.

© Discovery Enterprises, Ltd.
Carlisle, Massachusetts

© Discovery Enterprises, Ltd., Carlisle, MA 1995
ISBN 1-878668-51-X paperback edition
Library of Congress Catalog Card Number 95-68766

10   9   8   7   6   5   4   3   2

Printed in the United States of America

Subject Reference Guide

Reconstruction: Binding the Wounds
edited by Cheryl A. Edwards
Civil War: Reconstruction — U.S. History
Andrew Johnson — U.S. History
Constitutional Amendments — U.S. History
Radical Republicans — U.S. History
Ku Klux Klan — U.S. History

Photo/Illustration Credits

Cover Art – Receiving rations at the Freedmen's Bureau,
Title Page (Cartoon), Members of the KKK (p. 36), Blanche K. Bruce (p. 41),
Portrait of Andrew Johnson (p. 47), and the Impeachment Committee (p. 48):
Courtesy of the Library of Congress.

Illustration by David Huckins (p. 58): From *W.E.B. DuBois: Crusader for
Peace.* Lowell, MA: Discovery Enterprises, Ltd., 1991.

Acknowledgments

JoAnne B. Weisman, copy editing
Nancy Myers, design and typesetting

Table of Contents

Foreword
by
Cheryl Edwards

"With malice toward none, with charity for all, with firmness in the right as God gives us to see the right, let us strive on to finish the work we are in, to bind up the nation's wounds, to care for him who shall have borne the battle and for his widow and orphan, to do all which may achieve and cherish a just and lasting peace among ourselves and with all nations."

— President Abraham Lincoln
From his second Inaugural Address

On April 9, 1865, General Robert E. Lee surrendered to General Ulysses S. Grant at the Appomattox Court House in Virginia. The Civil War, which had lasted for four long years, had finally ended. Everyone agreed that both sides had suffered many losses. The War brought an end to slavery and a promise to restore the Union, but it left many complicated issues to resolve. The South's economy had been destroyed, and its people were hungry and homeless. President Lincoln wanted to restore the Union as quickly and as fairly as possible. However, political factions in Congress had their own agendas to promote. Political bickering divided the country and turned the Reconstruction process into another battleground.

Helping the South's homeless and hungry was the government's most urgent problem. The South's infrastructure had been totally destroyed. Cities had been burned to the ground, and railways, roads, and bridges were impassable. There were severe shortages of raw materials and manpower which hindered rebuilding efforts. Poverty and suffering touched all social classes. Wealthy aristocratic plantation owners lost everything, and most were little better off than the freed slaves who had once worked their fields. The freed slaves, who had been emancipated in 1863, were among the most destitute of the population. They were illiterate, homeless, and without any immediate hope for better opportunities. The War had totally paralyzed the South.

To help administer emergency relief to the South, the Congress created the Freedmen's Bureau. Among its many responsibilities were feeding the hungry, locating temporary housing, setting up schools, helping the freed slaves rebuild their lives, and looking after abandoned lands. Missionaries, churches, and thousands of volunteers supplemented the Bureau's sparse funding. Some white southerners criticized the Freedmen's Bureau, and accused its volunteers of creating racial tension between freedmen and their former masters. Others accused the Bureau of raising false hopes among the freedmen, many of whom retained the notion that the government was going to give them free land and a mule. Many freedmen also thought that they would never have to work for white people again. These rumors swept through the South and added to the confusion.

The extension of emergency relief was just a temporary bandaid. The President now had the ominous task of helping the South rebuild its economy and working out a plan to restore the Union. It did not take long for conflicts to erupt between the Congress and the President over which branch had the Constitutional power to set the terms of Reconstruction.

President Lincoln was a moderate Republican and a strong leader. Lincoln remained open-minded about the Reconstruction process, and welcomed ideas from fellow politicians. In 1863, Lincoln introduced his Presidential Plan of Reconstruction known as the "Ten Percent Plan". First, the plan offered a full pardon to all southerners who would agree to take an oath of allegiance to the Union and accept all of its laws. Secondly, Lincoln promised that a state could gain re-admittance to the Union and begin to form a new government when ten percent of the voters who voted in the 1860 election had taken the oath of allegiance.

Lincoln's Reconstruction Plan came up against opposition in Congress. A group of Republicans called the "Radical Republicans" voiced their dissent. Their leaders were Sen. Charles Sumner of Massachusetts and Rep. Thaddeus Stevens of Pennsylvania, both of whom wanted harsher conditions inflicted on the South. They questioned the loyalty of former Confederates, and their willingness to give political equality to African Americans.

Congressional support for the Radical Republicans resulted in the passage of the Wade-Davis Bill in 1864, which gave Congress the power to restore the Union. Lincoln refused to sign the bill.

President Lincoln did not live long enough to find out if his Reconstruction plan would have been successful. He was assassinated by John Wilkes Booth on April 14, 1865. Lincoln's death left the nation in shock. Both the North and South mourned his passing. Politicians worried that without Lincoln's moderate approach, Reconstruction was in jeopardy. Lincoln's successor, Andrew Johnson, was a Democrat who was not well respected by Congress. His stubborn attitude and unwillingness to compromise made him many political enemies. Johnson, who was also a southerner, still believed that African Americans were an inferior race, and did not support efforts to secure their civil rights.

President Johnson did carry out the major points of Lincoln's Plan for Reconstruction, and for a while, Reconstruction followed a moderate course. The former Confederate States wrote new Constitutions and organized new governments, but they were unwilling to guarantee African Americans their civil rights. They also inacted some unfavorable laws that made President Johnson's Reconstruction Plan look bad.

Many white southerners did not like all the changes that had been forced upon them by the Union government. They especially disliked the fact that African Americans were gaining power. The southern states implemented a solution to their growing social dilemma by creating a set of reactionary laws called "black codes," similar to the old slave codes. These laws were a way of denying African Americans their civil rights.

Source: Excerpted from *Cobblestone*, May, 1987 issue: Reconstruction, © 1987, Cobblestone Publishing, Inc., 7 School Street, Peterborough, NH 03458. Reprinted by permission of the publisher.

... several southern state legislatures enacted laws, called Black Codes, which were designed to keep blacks illiterate, unskilled, propertyless agricultural workers. The codes were adopted in 1865-1866 by the provisional governments that President Andrew Johnson set up in the South and reflected how confused some white persons were about the legal status of the ex-slaves at the end of the war.

In Mississippi, one of the leaders in passing the Black Codes, black persons under age eighteen who were orphans or whose parents could not support them had to work as apprentices to white persons, preferably their former owners. A black person who left a white employer without permission could be arrested and unless he or she paid a fine, could be required to work without wages for that employer. No black could practice a skilled trade without a license, possess a weapon, or buy or rent farmland.

In Louisiana, all black agricultural laborers were required to make one-year contracts with white landowners during the first ten days of January. Blacks could not leave their place of employment without permission. Blacks who refused to work for an employer were to be arrested and forced to work for the town without pay until they agreed to go back to their job[s].

In South Carolina, blacks had to get a special license if they wanted to do any type of work besides agricultural labor. Black employees who did not work as well as their white employers thought they should could be fined fifty dollars and forced to work six months without pay.

....

... Many of the men elected to the southern states legislatures after the Civil War had been Confederate leaders during the Civil War. They had a difficult time accepting the South's defeat, and their Black Codes were a way of maintaining control over the black population.

The Black Codes were denounced throughout the North; the Freedmen's Bureau issued regulations that nullified them. Eventually in the South, more open-minded politicians were elected to legislatures, where they managed to do away with the Black Codes. But the Black Codes continue to be a reminder of the complex problems associated with Reconstruction and the special burdens placed on the newly freed black men and women.

The Radical Republicans were very unhappy at the way Reconstruction had been proceeding under Johnson's guidance. Unlike Johnson, they wanted the Southern states to guarantee civil and political rights for African Americans. The fact that the southern governments had created the black codes proved to the Republicans that Congress needed to step in and take over the Reconstruction process. The stage was set for a showdown between the Radical Republicans and the President.

At the opening of the thirty-ninth Congress in 1865, the Radical Republicans were looking for a way to promote their agenda. To dramatize their point, they refused to seat the new southern Congressmen. They created a Joint Congressional Committee, made up of six Senators and nine Representatives, which was formed to take testimony, to examine the progress of Johnson's Reconstruction Plan, and to determine whether or not the Southern states should be represented in Congress. By using this tactic, the Radical Republicans were hoping to regain control, and institute their own plan.

In an effort to force the states to guarantee African Americans their civil rights, the Congress passed the Fourteenth Amendment, which gave African Americans full citizenship. They required the Southern states to ratify the Amendment as a condition for gaining re-admittance. Only Tennessee ratified it.

The election of 1866 gave the Radical Republicans a two-thirds majority in both houses. They no longer had to worry about a Presidential veto. In 1867, the Congress passed the Reconstruction Acts. The plan divided the southern states into military districts, and required them to form new governments, write new constitutions, give African American males the right to vote and hold office, deny political rights to ex-Confederate officials, and ratify the Fourteenth Amendment. Each state abided by these conditions, and, over time, they all gained re-admittance to the Union.

Although the Radical Republicans held a majority in Congress, they feared that President Johnson would not support the Congressional Reconstruction Plan. Those in favor of impeachment found a way to reduce the President's power, and set him up to commit an impeachable offense. Congress passed the Tenure of Office Act, which required the Senate's consent before the President could dismiss an important civil officer. Johnson, who enjoyed confrontation, and thought that the law was unconstitutional, decided to put the Congress to a test. He dismissed his Secretary of War Edwin Stanton on the grounds that Stanton sympathized with the Radical Republicans. The House of Representatives immediately voted to impeach the President.

Chief Justice Salmon Chase presided over Johnson's Senate trial, which lasted about two months. The Radical Republicans were fuming when the trial concluded with a not guilty verdict. Public opinion and support from moderate Republicans turned against the Radicals.

In an effort to regain the public's trust in the up-coming election, Republicans nominated former war hero Ulysses S. Grant for President. Grant denounced the Radicals and their support of civil rights for African Americans. He won the 1868 election by a slim margin, ironically with the help of the African American vote.

After the election, the Radicals introduced the Fifteenth Amendment, which officially gave African American men the right to vote. Although the states ratified the Amendment, the Radicals never regained their lost power. However, their Reconstruction policies did help rebuild the South, and placed many Radical Republicans in control of state governments.

The Reconstruction governments are often maligned for their corrupt practices and lavish spending. Some blamed the problems of the Reconstruction governments on carpetbaggers and scalawags. Carpetbaggers were northerners who came South to fill political positions in the Reconstruction governments that would normally have been filled by southerners. Many southern men had been stripped of their political rights and were not permitted to hold elected office. Scalawags, southerners who earned a reputation as ruthless fortune-seekers, cooperated with northerners.

Despite the criticism heaped on the Reconstruction governments, many individuals contributed to the South's recovery. For the first time, the Reconstruction governments elected African Americans like Hiram R. Revels and Blanche K. Bruce to the U.S. Senate, and Benjamin Turner and Josiah Walls to the House of Representatives. Others were elected to state and local positions. Reconstruction governments reformed public education and taxes, wrote new state Constitutions, and abolished imprisonment for debt.

Most white southerners resented interference from northerners in their affairs. Some were ex-Confederates who had lost their political rights, others were racists who did not want African Americans assuming political power. Their bitterness led them to form secret societies to stop blacks from voting and running for public office. The most well-known was the Ku Klux Klan.

Congress passed the Force Acts which gave the President the right to use military control to stop KKK activities. In 1872, the Congress also passed the Amnesty Act, which reinstated the political rights of ex-Confederate officials. The KKK's activities were somewhat curtailed and white southerners were given the chance of participating in their state governments again.

During the 1870's, Radical Reconstruction governments in the South were gradually replaced by governments led by white southerners. The Radical leaders Charles Sumner and Thaddeus Stevens had died. Northerners, growing tired of trying to calm the tensions between the races, thought it best to let the southerners work out their own problems. After the presidential election of 1877, President Rutherford B. Hayes pulled out the remaining troops from the South. Reconstruction had officially ended, but its legacy created more problems than it had attempted to solve.

In the postwar South, there were few economic opportunities for uneducated African Americans. Many became sharecroppers, working for landowners, who provided tools, seed, a plot of land, and a place to live in return for labor. The sharecropper also received a percentage of the crops that he grew each year. Sharecroppers lived in a world of revolving credit and debt. Very few had the opportunity of escaping their economic bondage, which was another form of slavery.

Racial tensions continued to grow in the years after Reconstruction. During the 1880's, southern governments passed laws which stripped African Americans of their civil rights and segregated public facilities. The racial hostilities in the South forced many blacks to migrate to northern cities.

In the following selection of journals, testimonies, reports, eye witness accounts, and historians' interpretations, you will learn how a nation tried to bind the wounds from the Civil War.

The South After the War

Mrs. Frances Butler Leigh's Account

*Frances Butler Leigh describes her travels through the South
after what she calls the "revolution" in these excerpts.*

Source: Frances Butler Leigh, *Ten Years on a Georgia Plantation
After the War* (London: R. Bentley and Son, 1883). From *THE SOUTH:
A Documentary History*, by Ina Woestemeyer Van Noppen (Princeton,
New Jersey: D. Van Nostrand Company, Inc., 1958).

The year after the war between the North and South,
I went to the South with my father to look after our property in Georgia and see what could be done with it.

The whole country had of course undergone a complete revolution. The changes that a four years' war must
bring about in any country would alone have been enough
to give a different aspect to everything; but at the South,
besides the changes brought about by the war, our slaves
had been freed; the white population was conquered,
ruined, and disheartened, unable for the moment to see
anything but ruin before as well as behind, too wedded to
the fancied prosperity of the old system to believe in any
possible success under the new. And even had the people
desired to begin at once to rebuild their fortunes, it would
have been in most cases impossible, for in many families
the young men had perished in the war, and the old men,
if not too old for the labour and effort it required to set the
machinery of peace going again, were beggared, and had
not even money enough to buy food for themselves and
their families, let alone their negroes, to whom they now
had to pay wages as well as feed them. ...

On March 22, 1866, my father and myself left
the North. The Southern railroads were many of them
destroyed for miles, not having been rebuilt since the
war, and it was very questionable how we were to get
as far as Savannah, a matter we did accomplish however,
in a week's time ... [We reached] Richmond at four
o'clock on Sunday morning. ...

....

I can hardly give a true idea of how crushed and sad
the people are. You hear no bitterness towards the North;
they are too sad to be bitter; their grief is overwhelming.
Nothing can make any difference to them now; the women
live in the past, and the men only in the daily present,
trying, in a listless sort of way, to repair their ruined
fortunes. They are like so many foreigners, whose only
interest in the country is their own individual business.
Politics are never mentioned, and they know and care less
about what is going on in Washington than in London.

....

...The fine houses have fallen to decay or been burnt
down; the grounds neglected and grown over with weeds;
the plantations left, with a few exceptions, to the negroes;
olive groves choked up with undergrowth; stately date-
palms ruthlessly burnt down by negroes to make room
for a small patch of corn, where there were hundreds of
acres, untilled, close at hand; a few solitary men eking
out an existence by growing fruit trees and cabbages, by
planting small patches of cotton or corn, by hunting deer,
or by selling whiskey to the negroes.

Problems of Daily Life

Both white southerners and freed slaves endured tremendous suffering after the war. The following passages describe the problems faced by both races.

Source: First excerpt, quoted from the *Senate Executive Document* No. 27, Congress, 1 Session. Second excerpt, quoted from the *Senate Executive Document* No. 2, 39 Congress, 1 Session.

... The general destitution has rendered many kindly disposed people unable to do anything for the negroes who were formerly their slaves, and who might be supposed to have some claims upon them for temporary assistance on that account, and there is much suffering among the aged and infirm, the sick and helpless, of this class of people... It is a common, and everyday sight in Randolph County, that of women and children, most of whom were formerly in good circumstances, begging for bread from door to door. Meat of any kind has been a stranger to many of their mouths for months. The drought cut off what little crops they hoped to save, and they must have immediate help or perish. ...

By far the greatest suffering exists among the whites. Their scanty supplies have been exhausted, and now they look to the government alone for support. Some are without homes of any description. This seems strange and almost unaccountable. Yet on one road leading to Talladega I visited four families, within fifteen minutes' ride of the town, who were living in the woods, with no shelter but pine boughs, and this in mid-winter. Captain Dean, who accompanied me, assured me that upon the other roads leading into town were other families similarly situated. These people have no homes. They were widows, with large families of small children. Other families, as provisions fail, will wander in for supplies, and I am fearful the result will be a camp of widows and orphans. If possible, it should be prevented; and yet I saw about thirty

15

persons for whom shelter must be provided, or death will speedily follow their present exposure and suffering. ...

When the war came to a close, the labor system of the South was already much disturbed. During the progress of military operations large numbers of slaves had left their masters and followed the columns of our armies; others had taken refuge in our camps; many thousands had enlisted in the service of the national government. Extensive settlements of negroes has been formed along the seaboard and the banks of the Mississippi, under the supervision of army officers and treasury agents, and the government was feeding the colored refugees, who could not be advantageously employed, in the contraband camps. Many slaves had been removed by their masters, as our armies penetrated the country, either to Texas or to the interior of George and Alabama. Thus a considerable portion of the laboring force had been withdrawn from its former employments. But a majority of the slaves remained on the plantations to which they belonged, especially in those parts of the country which were not touched by the war, and where, consequently, the emancipation proclamation was not enforced by the military power. When ... the report went ... out that their liberation was ... a fixed fact, large numbers of colored people left the plantations; many flocked to our military posts and camps to obtain the certainty of their freedom, and others walked away merely for the purpose of leaving the place on which they had been held in slavery, and because they could now go with impunity. Still others, and their number was by no means inconsiderable, remained with their former masters and continued their work on the field, but under new and as yet unsettled conditions, and under the agitating influence of a feeling of restlessness. ... The country found itself thrown into that confusion which is naturally inseparable from a change so great and so sudden ...

Economic Disaster

Historian Walter Lynwood Fleming described the South's desperate economic conditions in the following selections.

Source: Walter Lynwood Fleming, *The Sequel of Appomattox: A Chronicle of the Reunion of the States* (New Haven: Yale University Press, 1919).

From Harper's Ferry to New Market, which is about eighty miles ... the country was almost a desert. ... We had no cattle, hogs, sheep, or horse or anything else. The fences were all gone. Some of the orchards were very much injured, but the fruit trees had not been destroyed. The barns were all burned; chimneys standing without houses, and houses standing without roof, or door, or window.

Much land was thrown on the market at low prices— three to five dollars an acre for land worth fifty dollars. The poorer lands could not be sold at all, and thousands of farms were deserted by their owners. Everywhere recovery from this agricultural depression was slow. ...

There were few stocks of merchandise in the South when the war ended, and Northern creditors had lost so heavily through the failure of Southern merchants that they were cautious about extending credit again. Long before 1865 all coin had been sent out in contraband trade through the blockade. That there was a great need of supplies from the outside world is shown by the following statement of General Boynton:

'Window-glass has given way to thin boards, in railway coaches and in the cities. Furniture is marred and broken, and none has been replaced for four years. Dishes are cemented in various styles, and half the pitchers have tin handles. A complete set of crockery is never seen, and in very few families is there enough to set a table. ... A

17

set of forks with whole tines is a curiosity. Clocks and
watches have nearly all stopped. ... Hair brushes and tooth
brushes have all worn out; combs are broken. ... Pins,
needles, and thread, and a thousand such articles, which
seem indispensable to housekeeping, are very scarce.
Even in weaving on the looms, corncobs have been sub-
stituted for spindles. Few have pocket knives. In fact,
everything that has heretofore been an article of sale at the
South is wanting now. At the tables of those who were
once esteemed luxurious providers you will find neither
tea, coffee, sugar, nor spices of any kind. Even candles,
in some cases, have been replaced by a cup of grease in a
piece of cloth is plunged for a wick.'

This poverty was prolonged and rendered more acute
by the lack of transportation. Horses, mules, wagons,
and carriages were scarce, the country roads were nearly
impassable, and bridges were in bad repair or had been
burned or washed away. Steamboats had almost disap-
peared from the rivers. Those which had escaped capture
as blockade runners had been subsequently destroyed or
were worn out. Postal facilities, which had been poor
enough during the last year of the Confederacy, were
entirely lacking for several months after the surrender.

....

The South faced the work of reconstruction not only
with a shortage of material and greatly hampered in the
employment even of that but still more with a shortage
of men. ...

... The poorer whites who had lost all were close to
starvation. In the white counties which had sent so large
a proportion of men to the army the destitution was most
acute. In many families the breadwinner had been killed
in war. After 1862 relief systems had been organized in
nearly all the Confederate States for the purpose of aiding
the poor whites, but these organizations were disbanded
in 1865. ...

....

Acute distress continued until 1867; after that year there was no further danger of starvation. Some of the poor whites, especially in the remote districts, never again reached a comfortable standard of living; some were demoralized by too much assistance; others were discouraged and left the South for the West or the North. But the mass of the people accepted the discipline of poverty and made the best of their situation.

The difficulties, however, that beset even the courageous and the competent were enormous. The general paralysis of industry, the breaking up of society, and poverty on all sides bore especially hard on those who had not previously been manual laborers. Physicians could get practice enough but no fees; lawyers who had supported the Confederacy found it difficult to get back into the reorganized courts because of the test oaths and the competition of "loyal" attorneys; and for the teachers there were few schools. We read of officers high in the Confederate service selling to Federal soldiers the pies and cakes cooked by their wives, of others selling fish and oysters which they themselves had caught, and of men and women hitching themselves to plows when they had no horse or mule.

Changed Conditions and Readjustment

Belle Kearney's Account

Belle Kearney describes how life changed for southern aristo-cratic plantation owners in the following excerpt.

Source: Belle Kearney, *A Slaveholder's Daughter* (New York: The Abbey Press, 1900).

Changed Conditions

The Federal government, in its emancipation act, had set afloat an army of aged and infirm negroes who were perfectly helpless, becoming paupers at once on receiving their freedom. So in addition to other burdens the white people were forced, in their extremity, to continue to care for these, as when they were slaves.

. . . .

As soon as father was physically strong enough to perform the trying duty, he went to the negro quarters on his plantation, assembled his slaves, and announced to them that they were free. There was no wild shout of joy or other demonstration of gladness. The deepest gloom prevailed in their ranks and an expression of mournful bewilderment settled upon their dusky faces.

They did not understand that strange, sweet word— freedom. Poor things! the English language had never brought to them the faintest definition of liberty—that most glorious gift of God. They were stunned. What were they to do Where should they go? What would become of them? Who would feed and clothe them, and care for them in sickness, when they went out from "marster" free?

Noticing their consternation and dumb sorrow, father told them that they might stay and work for him as hired hands. Some of them did, but the majority drifted away, and finally all.

Readjustment

It seemed impossible for father and mother to realize the terrible changes that had come into their fortunes. They continued to live extravagantly for the first few years after the war, keeping the same number of house-servants and giving them exorbitant wages; also to the field-hands who were hired by the month. After awhile the last dollar was spent and the last servant dismissed. The land that had yielded bountiful harvests worked by the slaves, now brought a pittance rented to the freed-men. The struggle for bread became hard both for the laborer and the land-owner. Affairs were growing desperate. Then mortgages were unhappily entered into, and the inevitable failure to meet them was followed by foreclosure. Of all our former possessions only four hundred acres of land, around the old home, were left us.

Among the many destructive agencies to the attainment of independence were the lien laws instituted in the South at the close of the civil war. Before a spool of thread or a pound of flour could be bought on credit the purchaser had to give a lien on available property—cattle, horses or land. Failing he mortgaged his unplanted crop for sup-plies during the year. The rate of interest as well as the merchant's profits on goods was enormous, usually as high as 100 or 200 per cent. At the end of the year the buyer found himself in debt or escaped with only the clothes on his back. ...

In the midst of the social and financial convulsions that surrounded us in those sad days, father stood facing the ruin about him with right hand hopelessly injured and depressed continually by a frail constitution. Mother's health was wretched; she was a martyr to neuralgia. Worst of all, neither of them knew how to work, nor how to manage so as to make a dollar, nor how to keep it after it was gained. ...

21

Lincoln's Ten Percent Plan

As early as 1863, President Lincoln had already outlined his plan for readmitting the Southern states into the Union. This plan, called the Ten Percent Plan, stated that if ten percent of the people who voted in the 1860 election took an oath of allegiance to the Union, the state would be readmitted. President Lincoln presented this plan in his third annual message, given on December 8, 1863. An excerpt follows.

Source: From *A Compilation of the Messages and Papers of the Presidents, 1789-1902,* by James D. Richardson (Washington, published by authority of Congress, 1902, Vol. VI).

... I, Abraham Lincoln, President of the United States, do proclaim, declare, and make known to all persons who have, directly or by implication, participated in the existing rebellion, except as hereinafter excepted, that a full pardon is hereby granted to them and each of them, with restoration of all rights of property, except as to slaves and in property cases where rights of third persons have intervened, and upon the condition that every such person shall take and subscribe an oath and thenceforward keep and maintain said oath inviolate, and which oath shall be registered for permanent preservation and shall be of the tenor and effect following, to wit:

I, ———————— ———————— , do solemnly swear, in presence of Almighty God, that I will henceforth faithfully support, protect, and defend the Constitution of the United States and the Union of the States thereunder; and that I will in like manner abide by and faithfully support all acts of Congress passed during the existing rebellion with reference to slaves, so long and so far as not repealed, modified, or held void by Congress or by decision of the Supreme Court; and that I will in like manner abide by and faithfully support all proclamations of the President made during the existing rebellion having reference to slaves, so long and so far as not modified or declared void by decision of the Supreme Court. So help me God.

The persons excepted from the benefits of the foregoing provisions are all who are or shall have been civil or diplomatic officers or agents of the so-called Confederate Government; all who have left judicial stations under the United States to aid in the rebellion; all who are or shall have been military or naval officers of the so-called Confederate Government above the rank of colonel in the army or of lieutenant in the navy; all who left seats in the United States Congress to aid the rebellion; all who resigned commissions in the Army or Navy of the United States and afterwards aided the rebellion; and all who have engaged in any way in treating colored persons, or white persons in charge of such, otherwise than lawfully as prisoners of war, and which persons may have been found in the United States service as soldiers, seamen, or in any other capacity.

And I do further proclaim, declare, and make known that whenever, in any of the States of Arkansas, Texas, Louisiana, Mississippi, Tennessee, Alabama, Georgia, Florida, South Carolina, and North Carolina, a number of persons, not less than one-tenth in number of the votes cast in such State at the Presidential election of the year A.D. 1860, each having taken the oath aforesaid, and not having since violated it, and being a qualified voter by the election law of the State existing immediately before the so-called act of secession, and excluding all others, shall reestablish a State government which shall be republican ..., such shall be recognized as the true government of the State. ...

....

... It may be proper to say ... that whether members sent to Congress from any State shall be admitted to seats constitutionally rests exclusively with the respective Houses, and not to any extent with the Executive. ...

Given under my hand at the city of Washington, the 8th day of December, A.D., 1863. ...

23

Andrew Johnson Carries On

Johnson's First Annual Message

After President Lincoln's assassination on April 14, 1865, Johnson had the enormous responsibility of carrying on the job of restoring the Union. Johnson's plan for Reconstruction closely followed the ideas set forth by President Lincoln. The following is taken from his first annual message on December 4, 1865.

... I have ... gradually and quietly, and by almost imperceptible steps, sought to restore the rightful energy of the General Government and of the States. To that end provisional governors have been appointed for the States, conventions called, governors elected, legislatures assembled, and Senators and Representatives chosen to the Congress of the United States. ...

The next step which I have taken to restore the constitutional relations of the States has been an invitation to them to participate in the high office of amending the Constitution. ... The evidence of sincerity in the future maintenance of the Union shall be put beyond any doubt by the ratification of the proposed amendment to the Constitution, which provides for the abolition of slavery forever within the limits of our country. ...

Good faith requires the security of the freedmen in their liberty and their property, their right to labor, and their right to claim the just return for their labor. ... The country is in need of labor, and the freedmen are in need of employment, culture, and protection. ... Let us encourage them to honorable and useful industry, where it may be beneficial to themselves and to the country. ...

Relief and Education

Freedmen's Bureau

The federal government created the Freedmen's Bureau to administer emergency assistance to former slaves and white southerners after the war. The Bureau's volunteers set up schools, fed the hungry, found temporary housing for the homeless, and helped the freed slaves adjust to their new lives. Journalist John T. Trowbridge from Massachusetts wrote about his observations of a school run by the Freedmen's Bureau. An excerpt from his work follows:

Source: Excerpted from *A Picture of the Desolated States and the Work of Restoration* by J.T. Trowbridge (Hartford, Conn., 1868).

There were three thousand pupils in the freedmen's schools. The teachers for these were furnished, here as elsewhere, chiefly by benevolent societies in the North. Such of the citizens as did not oppose the education of the blacks, were generally silent about it. Nobody said of it, "That is freedom! That is what the Yankees are doing for them.!"

Visiting these schools in nearly all the Southern States, I did not hear of the white people taking any interest in them. With the exception of here and there a man or woman inspired by Northern principles, I never saw or heard of a Southern citizen, male or female, entering one of those humble school-rooms. ...

The wonder with me was, how these "best friends" could be so utterly careless of the intellectual and moral interests of the freedmen. For my own part, I could never enter one of those schools without emotion. They were often held in old buildings and sheds good for little else. There was not a school room in Tennessee furnished with appropriate seats and desks. I found a similar condition of things in all the States. The pews of colored churches, or plain benches in the vestries, or old chairs with boards laid across them in some loft over a shop, or out-of-doors on the grass in summer,—such was the usual scene of the freedmen's schools.

....

... I never visited one of any size in which there were not two or three or half a dozen children so nearly white that no one would have suspected the negro taint. From these, the complexion ranges through all the indescribable mixed hues, to the shining iron black of a few pure-blooded Africans, perhaps not more in number than the seemingly pure-blooded whites. The younger the generation, the lighter the average skin; by which curious fact one perceives how fast the race was bleaching under the "peculiar" system or slavery.

Mary Ames' Diary

As a young woman from Boston, Mary Ames volunteered to become a teacher. In 1865, she went to South Carolina to teach former slaves how to read and write.

Source: Mary Ames, *From A New England Woman's Diary in Dixie in 1865* (Springfield, 1906).

The school was in a building once used as a billiard room, which accommodated a large number of pupils. We often had a hundred and twenty, and when word went forth that supplies had come, the number increased. Indeed, it was so crowded that we told the men and women they must stay away to leave space for the children, as we considered teaching them more important. ...

When we made out the school report to send to Boston, we were surprised that out of the hundred, only three children knew their age, nor had they the slightest idea of it; one large boy told me he was "Three months old." The next day many of them brought pieces of wood or bits of paper with straight marks made on them to show how many years they had lived. One boy brought a family record written in a small book.

In January smallpox broke out among the soldiers quartered on our place. Many of our scholars took it, and we closed the school for five weeks. We escaped, although in continual danger, for the negroes, even when repulsively sick, were so eager for our gifts of clothing that they forced their way to our very bedrooms, and our carryall, drawn by men, was used to carry the patients to the improvised hospital. ... When on Monday, February twenty-sixth, we began school again, we had thirteen pupils. One of them, when asked if there was smallpox at her plantation, answered, "No, the last one died Saturday." On the third day one hundred children had come back.

Radical Republicans Demand Redistribution of Wealth

Thaddeus Stevens' Speech

Opposition to President Johnson's lenient Reconstruction Plan sprung up in Congress. A group of Republicans known as the Radical Republicans put forth their own version of a plan. The two leaders of the Radical Republicans were Congressman Thaddeus Stevens of Pennsylvania and Senator Charles Sumner of Massachusetts. They proposed a harsh set of polices that the Southern States had to fulfill in order for them rejoin the Union. In 1865, Thaddeus Stevens made a speech in Lancaster, Pennsylvania, where he promoted the idea of confiscating property in the South and redistributing it among freed slaves. The following is an excerpt from his speech.

Source: Richard Nelson Current, *Old Thad Stevens* (Madison: University of Wisconsin Press, 1942).

... We hold it to be the duty of the Government to inflict condign punishment on the rebel belligerents, and so weaken their hands that they can never again endanger the Union; and so reform their municipal institutions as to make them republican in spirit as well as in name.

We especially insist that the property of the chief rebels should be seized and appropriated to the payment of the National debt, caused by the unjust and wicked war which they instigated.

How can such punishments be inflicted and such forfeitures produced without doing violence to established principles.

Two positions have been suggested.

1st—To treat those States as never having been out of the Union. ...

2nd—To accept the position in which they placed themselves as severed from the Union; an independent government *de facto,* and an enemy alien to be dealt with according to the laws of war. ...

In reconstruction ... no reform can be effected in the Southern States if they have never left the Union. But reformation *must* be effected; the foundation of their institutions, both political, municipal and social must be broken up and *relaid,* or all our blood and treasure have been spent in vain. This can only be done by treating and holding them as a conquered people. Then all things which we can desire to do, follow with logical and legitimate authority. As conquered territory Congress would have full power to legislate for them. ... They would be held in a territorial condition until they are fit to form State Constitutions, republican in fact not in form only, and ask admission into the Union as new States. ...

We propose to confiscate all the estate of every rebel belligerent whose estate was worth $10,000, or whose land exceeded two hundred acres in quantity. Policy if not justice would require that the poor, the ignorant, and the coerced should be forgiven. They followed the example of their wealthy and intelligent neighbors. The rebellion would never have originated with them. Fortunately those who would thus escape form a large majority of the people, though possessing but a small portion of the wealth. The proportion of those exempt compared with the punished would be I believe about nine tenths.

The Joint Committee on Reconstruction

At the opening of the thirty-ninth Congress in 1865, the Radical Republicans were looking for a way to promote their agenda. They wanted to weaken and destroy President Johnson's Reconstruction plans. To dramatize their point, they chose not to let the new Southern Congressmen take their seats. They then formed a Joint Congressional Committee made up of six Senators and nine Representatives. This Committee was asked to study the Reconstruction issues, and then determine if the ex-Confederate States were entitled to be represented in Congress. The Radical Republicans believed that Congress should make Reconstruction policy, not the President.

These testimonies were taken from the Joint Committee on Reconstruction.

Source: Hans L. Trefousse, *Background For Radical Reconstruction* (Boston: Little Brown and Co., 1970). Excerpts taken from the *Hearings of the Joint Committee on Reconstruction, the Select Committee on the Memphis Riots and Massacres, and the Select Committee on the New Orleans Riots — 1866 and 1867.*

Testimony of Homer A. Cook

Q. What effect his President Johnson's liberal policy in granting pardons and amnesties to rebels had upon the minds of the secessionists there; has it made them more or less favorable to the government of the United States? —*A.* I can, perhaps, better answer that question by saying that every unconditional Union man of my acquaintance in that state is opposed to that policy.

Q. How do the secessionists feel about it?—*A. They* claim the President as their friend in that matter.

. . . .

Q. How do they speak of the majority in the two houses of Congress?—*A.* In terms of deep and malignant hatred.

Q. What are some of the epithets they apply to them, if they apply any?—*A.* They are spoken of as radicals, who would ruin their country if they cannot rule it.

Testimony of the Rev. James W. Hunnicutt

Rev. James W. Hunnicutt was one of the most radical southerners of the Reconstruction Era.

Q. What is the effect of President Johnson's policy of reconstruction there?—*A.* ... They are all in favor of President Johnson's policy of reconstruction. As soon as they get their ends served by him they would not touch him, but he is their man now. They say that in 1868 the South will be a unit, and that with the help of the copperhead party of the North they will elect a President. They do not care to have slavery back, but they will try and make the federal government pay them for their slaves. A man from Virginia told me today that they would be paid for their Negroes. This gentleman lost forty Negroes. This is their idea; they do not want slavery back, but they want to be paid for their slaves. They say that unless you accept their debt they will repudiate yours. They say they are not interested in this government.

....

Q. They propose to get back into the Union for the purpose of restoring the Constitution?—*A.* Yes, sir, and the testimony of the Negroes will not be worth a snap of your finger, and all this is done for policy. A Negro can come and give his testimony, and it passes for what it is worth with the courts. They can do what they please with it; there are judges, the lawyers, and the jury against the Negro, and perhaps every one of them is sniggering and laughing while the Negro is giving his testimony.

Q. Has not the liberal policy of President Johnson in granting pardons and amnesties rather tended to soothe and allay their feelings towards the government of the United States?—*A.* No, sir, not towards the government of the United States nor towards the Union men.

Testimony of James D. B. DeBow

James D. B. DeBow, a southern writer and editor, gave testimony to the Joint Committee on Reconstruction on the treatment of African Americans in southern cities.

Q. What is your opinion of the necessity or utility of the Freedmen's Bureau, or of any agency of that kind? —*A.* I think if the whole regulation of the Negroes, or freedmen, were left to the people of the communities in which they live, it will be administered for the best interest of the Negroes as well as of the white men. I think there is a kindly feeling on the part of the planters towards the freedmen. They are not held at all responsible for anything that has happened. They are looked upon as the innocent cause. In talking with a number of planters, I remember some of them telling me they were succeeding very well with their freedmen, having got a preacher to preach to them and a teacher to teach them, believing it was for the interest of the planter to make the Negro feel reconciled; for, to lose his services as a laborer for even a few months would be very disastrous. The sentiment prevailing is, that it is for the interest of the employer to teach the Negro, to educate his children, to provide a preacher for him, and to attend to his physical wants. And I may say I have not seen any exception to that feeling the South. Leave the people to themselves, and they will manage very well. The Freedmen's Bureau, or any agency to interfere between the freedman and his former master, is only productive of mischief. There are constant appeals from one to the other and continual annoyances. It has a tendency to create dissatisfaction and disaffection on the part of the laborer, and is in every respect in its result most unfavorable to the system of industry that is now being organized under the new order of things in the South. I do not think there is any difference of opinion upon this subject.

....

Q. What, in your opinion, is to be the effect upon the blacks?—*A.* I think it will be disastrous to them. I judge that because of the experience of other countries, and not from any experience we have had ourselves. I judge by their shiftless character, and their disposition to crowd into the cities. It is what I see all over the South. You will find large numbers of them in every city, crowded together in miserable shanties, eking out a very uncertain subsistence; and, so far, the mortality has been very great among them. They were not disposed to enter upon any regular work before the first of January. They were confident in the expectation that the lands were to be divided among them up to that time. But after the first of January they became satisfied they were not to get the lands, and they very generally went to work.

Q. What arrangements are generally made among the landholders and the black laborers in the South?—*A.* I think they generally get wages. A great many persons, however, think it better to give them an interest in the crops. That is getting to be very common.

Q. What do you find the disposition of the people as to the extension of civil rights to the blacks—the right to sue and enforce their contracts and to hold property, real and personal, like white people?—*A.* I think there is a willingness to give them every right except the right of suffrage. ...

Q. Suppose the Negroes were to vote now, what would be the influences operating upon them as to the exercise of that vote?—*A.* The Negro would be apt to vote with his employer if he was treated well. That is his character. They generally go with their employer; but it is probable they would be tampered with a great deal. There would be emissaries sent among them to turn their minds; so that, although I understand some prominent men think the Negro would generally vote with his master, I doubt it. ...

Congressional Reconstruction Policy

The Joint Committee drafted a plan to readmit the ex-Confederate States. At first, their plan required that the Southern states ratify the Fourteenth Amendment to gain re-admittance. However, this policy proved unsuccessful. After nearly a year, only Tennessee had ratified the Amendment. The Radical Republicans in Congress proposed another plan. Over a Presidential veto, Congress passed the Reconstruction Act, which divided the South into military districts. This plan required that the Southern states write new constitutions and form new governments, before they could be considered for re-admission. By 1870, all the Southern states had been readmitted. Federal troops remained in the South until 1877, to protect the civil rights of "Negroes".

In 1867, Francis Butler Leigh wrote a letter in which she stated her views on the Congressional Reconstruction Policy.

Source: Frances Butler Leigh, *Ten Years on a Georgia Plantation After the War* (London: R. Bentley and Son, 1883).

We are, I am afraid, going to have terrible trouble by-an-by with the negroes, and I see nothing but gloomy prospects for us ahead. The unlimited power that the war has put into the hands of the present Government at Washington seems to have turned the heads of the party now in office, and they don't know where to stop. The whole South is settled and quiet, and the people too ruined and crushed to do anything against the government, even if they felt so inclined, and all are returning to their former peaceful pursuits, trying to rebuild their fortunes, and thinking of nothing else. Yet the treatment we receive from the Government becomes more and more severe every day, the last act being to divide the South into five military districts, putting each under the command of a United States General, doing away with all civil courts and law. ...

A Southerner's Point of View

A look at Reconstruction from a white southerner's point of view is offered in this excerpt.

Source: Thomas Nelson Page, "The Southern People During Reconstruction," *Atlantic Monthly,* Vol. 88, September, 1901.

The worst that the people of the South anticipated was being brought back into the union with their property gone and their wounds yet smarting. The sense of defeat, together with the loss of property by force of arms, which left them almost universally impoverished, and the disruption of their social system, was no little burden for them to bear; but it was assumed bravely enough, and they went to work with energy and courage, and even with a certain high-heartedness. They started in on the plantations, where by reason of the disorganization of all labor they were needed, as wagoners or ploughmen or blacksmiths. They went to the cities, and became brakemen or street-car drivers, or watchmen or porters. Or they sought employ on public works in any capacity; men who had been generals even taking places as axemen or teamsters till they could rise to be superintendents and presidents. But they had peace and hope.

. . . .

The Freedmen's Bureau and its work soon had the whole South in a ferment. The distribution of rations relieved the slaves, but misled them into thinking that the government would support them, whether they worked or not. ...

. . . .

The white race ... were not allowed the franchise again until they had assented to giving the black race absolute equality in all matters of civil right. This the leaders of the other side vainly imagined would perpetuate their power, and for a time it almost promised to do so.

Members of the KKK in 1868

The result of the new regime thus established in the South was such a riot of rapine and rascality as had never been known in the history of this country, and hardly ever in the history of the world. ... The states were given over to pillage at the hands of former slaves, led largely by adventurers whose only aim was to gratify their vengeance of their cupidity.

Unable to resist openly the power of the National government that stood behind the carpet-bag governments of the states, the people of the South resorted to other means which proved for a time more or less effective. Secret societies were formed, which, under such titles as the "Ku Klux Klan," the "Knights of the White Camellia," the "White Brotherhood," etc., played a potent and, at first, it would seem, a beneficial part in restraining the excesses of the newly exalted leaders and their excited levies.

Wherever masked and ghostly riders appeared, the frightened negroes kept under cover. The idea spread with rapidity over nearly all the South, and the secret organizations, known among themselves as the "Invisible Empire," were found to be so dangerous to the continued power of the carpet-bag governments, and in places so menacing to their representatives personally, that the aid of the National government was called in to suppress them.

In a short time every power of the government was in motion, or ready to be set in motion, against them. "Ku Klux Acts" were passed; presidential proclamations were issued; the entire machinery of the United States courts was put in operation; the writ of habeas corpus was suspended in those sections where the Ku Klux were most in evidence, and Federal troops were employed. ...

The Ku Klux Klan

From testimony taken at a Senate Hearing on terrorist activity, Elias Hall recounts his terrifying encounter with the Ku Klux Klan in South Carolina.

Source: Ina Woestemeyer Van Noppen, *THE SOUTH: A Documentary History* (Princeton, New Jersey: D. Van Nostrand Company, Inc., 1958). From "A Report of the Joint Committee to Inquire into the Conditions of Affairs in the Late Insurrectionary States," Washington, 1872, Vol. III.

Question. State whether at any time men in disguise have come to the place where you live, and, if so, what they did and said. First, state when it was.

Answer. On the night of the 5th of last May, after I had heard a great deal of what they had done in that neighborhood, they came. It was between 12 and 1 o'clock at night, when I was awakened and heard the dogs barking, and something walking, very much like horses. As I had often laid awake listening for such persons, for they had been all through the neighborhood, and disturbed all men and many women, I supposed that it was them. They came in a very rapid manner, and I could hardly tell whether it was the sound of horses or men. At last they came to my brother's door, which is in the same yard, and broke open the door and attacked his wife, and I heard her screaming and moaning. I could not understand what they said, for they were talking in an outlandish and unnatural tone, which I had heard they generally used at a negro's house. I heard them knocking around in her house. I was lying in my little cabin in the yard. At last I heard them have her in the yard. She was crying, and the Ku-Klux were whipping her to make her tell where I lived. I heard her say, "Yon is her house." She has told me since that they first asked who had taken me out of her house. They said, "Where's Elias?" She said "He doesn't stay here; yon is his house." They were then in the yard, and I had heard them strike her five or six licks when I heard her say this. Some one then hit my door. It flew open. One ran in the house, and stopping about the middle of the house, which is a small cabin, he turned around as it seemed to me as I lay there, awake, and said "Who's here?" Then I knew they would take me, and I answered, "I am here." He shouted for joy, as it seemed, "Here he is! Here he is! We have found him!" and he threw the bedclothes off of me and caught me by one arm, while another man took me by the other and they carried me into the yard between the houses, my brother's and mine, and put me on the ground beside a boy. The first thing they asked me was, "Who did that burning? Who burned our houses?" gin-houses, dwelling-houses and such. Some had been burned in the neighborhood. I told them it was not me; I could not burn houses; it was unreasonable to ask me. Then they hit me with their fists, and said I did it, I ordered it. ... After they had staid in the house for a considerable time, they came back to where I lay and asked if I wasn't afraid at all. They pointed pistols at me all

around my head once or twice, as if they were going to
shoot me, telling me they were going to kill me, wasn't
I ready to die? and willing to die? didn't I preach? that
they came to kill me—all the time pointing pistols at me.
The second time they came out of the house, after plundering the house, searching for letters, they came at me with
these pistols, and asked if I was ready to die. I told them
that I was not exactly ready; that I would rather live; that
I hoped they would not kill me that time. They said they
would: I had better prepare. One caught me by the leg
and hurt me, for my leg for forty years has been drawn
each year, more and more year by year, and I made moan
when it hurt so. One said "G-d d—n it, hush!" He had
a horsewhip, and he told me to pull up my shirt and he
hit me. He told me at every lick "Hold up your shirt."
I made a moan every time he cut with the horsewhip. I
reckon he struck me eight cuts right off the hip bone; it
was almost the only place he could hit my body, my legs
are so short—all my limbs drawn up and withered away
with pain. I saw one of them standing over me or by
me motion to them to quit. They all had disguises on.
I then thought they would not kill me. One of them
then took a strap and buckled it around my neck and
said, "Let's take him to the river and drown him." ...
With that one of them went into the house where my
brother and my sister-in-law lived, and brought her to
pick me up. As she stooped down to pick me up one
of them struck her, and as she was carrying me into the
house another struck her with a strap. She carried me into the house and laid me on the bed. Then they gathered
around and told me to pray for them. I tried to pray. They
said "Don't you pray against Ku-Klux, but pray that God
may forgive Ku-Klux. Don't pray against us. Pray that
God may bless and save us."

Black Reconstructionists

Blacks in Office

During Reconstruction, African Americans were elected to public office. However, public opinion was not in their favor. Many whites argued that their lack of education and skills prevented them from carrying out their political jobs effectively. Despite the disadvantages of a lack of education and experience, black lawmakers were successful at helping to draft new state constitutions. These constitutions withstood the test of time, and did not need to be rewritten until long after Reconstruction had ended.

The first African American to be elected to the United States Senate was Hiram R. Revels of Mississippi. He was elected by the Mississippi legislature to serve the unexpired term of Jefferson Davis. Many Senators expressed opposition to the seating of Revels. They cited the fact that Revels did not meet the constitutional requirement of being a U.S. citizen for nine years prior to becoming a United States Senator. According to the law, African Americans had just recently attained citizenship, a point used by critics to try to block Revels from being seated.

In the following passages taken from debates in the U.S. Senate and House of Representatives, Senator Garret Davis of Kentucky and Senator James Nye of Nevada express their opposing opinions on seating a "Negro" in the United States Senate.

Source: Emma Lou Thornbrough, ed., *Black Reconstructionists* (Englewood Cliffs, NJ: Prentice-Hall, 1972).

Mr. President, this is certainly a morbid state of affairs. Never before in the history of this government has a colored man been elected to the Senate of the United States. To-day for the first time one presents himself and asks admission to a seat in it. How does he get here? Did he come here by the free voices by the spontaneous choice of the free people of Mississippi? No, sir; no. The sword of a military dictator has opened the way for his easy march to the Senate of the United States. ...

Senator James Nye of Nevada replies to Davis of Kentucky.

Sir, it seems to me that this is the crowning glory of a long series of measures. It seems to me that this is the day long looked for, when we put into practical effect the theory that has existed as old as man. We say that all men are brothers; whatever their color all are subject to the same law, and all are eligible to fill any place within the gift of the people.

Is the honorable Senator from Kentucky afraid to enter in the race for future glory with these colored me? ...

Like Revels, Blanche K. Bruce was elected a Senator from Mississippi in 1875. After escaping slavery in Virginia, Bruce headed North and attended Oberlin College, prior to beginning his term in office.

An Outsider Considers Black Reconstructionists

Sometimes an outsider's opinion of a country's political problems gives a more objective view of the situation. This selection offers the viewpoint of Sir George Campbell, an English traveler, who toured the Southern states after the fall of the Republican governments. It presents Campbell's views on black Reconstructionists.

Source: Sir George Campbell, *White and Black. The Outcome of a Visit to the United States* (New York: 1879). From *Black Reconstructionists,* by Emma Lou Thornbrough, ed., (Englewood Cliffs, NJ: Prentice-Hall, 1972).

During the last dozen years the negroes have had a very large share of political education. Considering the troubles and the ups and downs that they have gone through, it is, I think, wonderful how beneficial this education has been to them, and how much these people, so lately in the most debased condition of slavery, have acquired independent ideas, and, far from lapsing into anarchy, have become citizens with ideas of law and property and order. The white serfs of European countries took hundreds of years to rise to the level which these negroes have attained in a dozen. ...

On the whole, then, I am inclined to believe that the period of Carpet-bag rule was rather a scandal than a very permanent injury. The black men used their victory with moderation, although the women were sometimes dangerous, and there was more pilfering than plunder on a scale permanently to cripple the State.

Carpetbaggers and Scalawags

Reconstruction governments were made up of African Americans, white southerners, and northerners. The northerners who went South to serve in the Reconstruction governments were called carpetbaggers. The term comes from the fact that they carried their belongings in large cloth bags. Most carpetbaggers were good people who wanted to help both blacks and whites. Some worked for the Freedmen's Bureau, others were businessmen who came to invest their money. Also, many ex-Union soldiers decided to stay and help rebuild the Southern states. Many white southerners resented the carpetbaggers for several reasons. Primarily, the white southerners disliked northerners running their governments, and disapproved of the carpetbaggers' acceptance of African Americans as their equals.

Scalawags were southern natives who worked with African Americans and white southerners for their own personal gain. Most wanted to make fast money and gain political power. They often took advantage of people and gained a reputation of being ruthless.

Horace Greeley Campaigns

In 1872, The Liberal Republicans nominated Horace Greeley, a newspaper editor, to run as their presidential candidate. Greeley ran against President Grant, a Republican. During the campaign, Grant was blamed for the failure of Reconstruction. Carpetbaggers were also blamed and were an easy target for critics. In this excerpt from a speech given by Horace Greeley in 1871, Greeley attacks carpetbaggers.

Source: Excerpted from the *Chicago Tribune,* which serialized the speech on June 14, July 18, 24, August 14, 26, 1872. From *Those Terrible Carpetbaggers,* by Richard Nelson Current (New York: Oxford University Press, 1988).

The thieving carpet-baggers are a mournful fact; they do exist there, and I have seen them. They are fellows who crawled down South in the track of our armies, generally at a very safe distance in the rear; some of them in sutler's wagons; some bearing cotton permits; some of them looking sharply to see what might turn up; and they remained there. They at once ingratiated themselves with the blacks, simple, credulous, ignorant men, very glad to welcome and to follow any whites who professed to be the champions of their rights. Some of them got elected Senators, others Representatives, some Sheriffs, some Judges, and so on. And there they stand, right in the public eye, stealing and plundering, many of them with both arms around negroes, and their hands in their rear pockets, seeing if they cannot pick a paltry dollar out of them.. ... What the Southern people see of us are these thieves, who represent the North to their jaundiced vision, and, representing it, they disgrace it. *They are the greatest obstacle to the triumph and permanent ascendancy of Republican principles at the South, and as such I denounce them.*

Albert Griffin: In Defense of Carpetbaggers

Albert Griffin, a Republican from Georgia, defended carpet-baggers in this selection.

Source: Excerpted from the *New York Times,* November 15, 1872; Albert Griffin, "The Infamous Carpet-bag Governments', *Kansas Magazine,* September 1872. From *Those Terrible Carpetbaggers,* by Richard Nelson Current (New York: Oxford University Press, 1988).

The negroes are Southern people—natives, mostly—and even the so-called carpet-baggers are as much entitled to be considered a part of the people as are a majority of the inhabitants of this State [Kansas] to be called Kan-

44

sans, or Carl Schurz [a leading Liberal, born in Germany, formerly a Wisconsinite] a Missourian. It seems strange indeed to hear recent settlers in the West quietly assume that those who have gone South since the war are not a part of the people where they reside, and have no political rights, except to pay taxes and vote for those who despise and revile them. But it is stranger still to try to realize that Horace Greeley, Theodore Tilton, and others with like record, in looking South for "the people," can now see none but ex-Rebels and their allies; that in their eyes the colored men they have pleaded for so eloquently, and the union soldiers they have so often, so justly and so highly praised, have suddenly become nobodys merely because the Republican party refused to be dictated to by a cabal of malcontents respecting the renomination of President Grant.

The Yazoo Banner, *a Democratic newspaper in Yazoo City, Mississippi, printed these verses from a song about carpetbaggers. The song mocks Charles Morgan, a Wisconsinite who came to Mississippi, and who was considered a "Yankee outcast" by the southern whites.*

Old Morgan came to the Southern land
With a little carpet-bag in his hand.
Old Morgan thought he would get bigger
By running a saw-mill with a nigger.

The chorus went, in part:

If you belong to the Ku Klux Klan,
Here's my heart and here's my hand.

Johnson's Impeachment Trial

Georges Clemenceau, an American correspondent for a French newspaper, covered the impeachment trial of President Johnson. The following excerpts include his impressions and view on the trial.

Source: Georges Clemenceau, *American Reconstruction 1865-1870 and the Impeachment of President Johnson* (New York: The Dial Press, 1928).

February 28, 1868. The black cloud has finally broken. The President called upon the lightning, and the lightning came. Andrew Johnson, President of the United States, has been impeached, and the Senate is preparing to pass judgment upon him. ...

....

... the Senate immediately adopted a resolution, declaring that the President has no authority to remove the Secretary of War from office. In the House of Representatives there was so much excitement that no one could make himself heard. The members collected in groups, sending out contradictory proposals from time to time, wondering how Mr. Johnson grew so daring. He must have weighed the consequences of his action, and he must know as well as anyone that he has openly violated the Tenure of Office Bill. It is no use arguing that he himself considers this law unconstitutional, because, until the Supreme Court has given its opinion, the President is bound to put into execution the laws which Congress passes. It is impossible to see what the President is driving at, for he knows that article 6 of this bill states that any removal from office or any appointment made contrary to the provisions of this law will be considered a high misdemeanor, and the Constitution states that the President can be disposed for high crimes and misdemeanors. ...

May 29, 1868. At last the President's trial is over. The seven renegades, as the organs of the radical party call their Senators who voted for acquittal, are in the most embarrassing position imaginable. ...

....

Andrew Johnson

Very fortunately, Mr. Johnson seems much cooled down and calmed. He is satisfied with having got off with a fright and will probably not attempt any new outbreaks. It is said that he is thinking of changing his cabinet, but this is not likely. Mr. Seward is, and will continue to be, Mr. Johnson's mentor. The influence, or at least the maneuvers, of the Secretary of State played a considerable part in the President's acquittal, and one does not shut the door of one's house on a man who has just saved one's life. Besides, nothing would ever fill up the gulf that yawns between Mr. Johnson and the radicals.

The wisest course would be to try, not to understand each other, since that could not be, but at least to live in peace side by side, for the few months which they still have to spend together. Both sides must understand this simple truth.

The impeachment committee

"The Civil War and the Constitution"

Amendments Passed

Source: Excerpted from *Cobblestone,* May, 1987 issue:
Reconstruction, © 1987, Cobblestone Publishing, Inc., 7 School Street,
Peterborough, NH 03458.

The Civil War caused more constitutional amendments to be passed than any other event in U.S. history.
Although the war had been fought to save the Union,
it also became the war to free the slaves. Many people
felt that this could be done by passing laws. But laws
can be changed, repealed, or even declared unconstitutional, whereas an amendment is part of the Constitution
and becomes the law of the land.

In 1865, the Thirteenth Amendment, which officially
abolished slavery, was passed by two-thirds of the House
and Senate and ratified by three-fourths of the states. The
newly freed slaves, however, had no place to go. Their
food, clothing, and housing had always been provided by
the plantation owners. Now they had to learn to live on
their own. In addition, some southern states passed Black
Codes, which regulated the activities of the blacks.

Although blacks were no longer slaves, they were
also not protected by the laws of the nation. So in 1866,
Congress passed the Fourteenth Amendment, which made
all persons born or naturalized in the United States citizens. ("Naturalized" means foreign born but given U.S.
citizenship.) The Fourteenth Amendment was ratified by
the states and became a part of the Constitution in 1868.

Section 1 of this amendment said that no state could
deprive a person of life, liberty, or property without due
process of law. In other words, a person was guaranteed

the right to a fair trial or jury of one's peers. The states also could not deny citizens equal protection under the law. In practice, this meant that any citizen would be protected regardless of race, color, or national origin.

Section 2 recognized that the end of slavery had nullified the three-fifths clause of the Constitution, under which five slaves had counted as three whites in fixing the number of representatives each state had in the House of Representatives. (The number of representatives from each state is based on the state's population.) Because whites and blacks now counted equally, the South gained representation in the House. This seemed unfair to the North, as the South now had more representatives than ever before. It seemed as though the South was being rewarded for having revolted against the U.S. government.

To pacify the northern states, section 2 provided that if a state denied the right to vote to any citizen of the United States, it would lose some of its congressional representatives. In other words, black males had to be given the right to vote or the state would lose the additional representatives it had received based on the number of blacks. Section 2 was not, however, enforced. Many southern states denied the vote to blacks, but Congress made no effort to punish them.

The Fourteenth Amendment also denied former officials of the Confederacy the right to hold office. In addition, it said that the U.S. government did not have to pay back the money private citizens had given to the Confederacy to buy weapons and uniforms for the South. At the same time, the federal government guaranteed that it would pay all debts incurred by the North during the war.

Although the Fourteenth Amendment officially ended racial discrimination through its due process and equal protection clauses, minorities in the United States would not have the political power to change things until they had the right to vote.

In 1870, the Fifteenth Amendment gave all males twenty-one and older, regardless of race, color, or previous condition of servitude, the right to vote. Again, many southern states found ways of getting around the law. They required that all voters take a literacy test (could they read and understand a part of the Constitution?). Voters also were required to pay a poll tax. Since many blacks could not read and did not have the money to pay the tax, they were denied their right to vote. Not until the Voting Rights Act of 1965 did all racial discrimination in voting, including literacy tests, come to an end.

The Thirteenth, Fourteenth, and Fifteenth amendments had far-reaching effects on all American citizens. They made sure that each of us would be treated fairly under the law, and they made it possible for everyone to vote for the candidates of his or her choice.

The amendment procedure has allowed us to make changes in U.S. government policy. What began as a Constitution to uphold the rights of the individual against the tyranny of the majority has, through amendments, become a document that grants authority to the majority, while respecting minority rights. Because of the possibility of adding amendments, the Constitution is still a living document, responsive to changing times and changing values.

Emancipation: A Gradual Process

The Thirteenth Amendment officially abolished slavery. However, emancipation created many problems for freed slaves. Many were homeless, hungry, and in need of jobs and an education. In the following excerpt, Walter Lynwood Fleming describes the emancipated slaves' plight.

Source: Walter Lynwood Fleming, *The Sequel of Appomattox: A Chronicle of the Reunion of the States* (New Haven: Yale University Press, 1919).

Emancipation was therefore a gradual process, and most of the negroes, through their widening experience on the plantation, with the armies, and in the colonies, were better fitted for freedom in 1865 than they had been in 1861. Even their years of bondage had done something for them, for they knew how to work and they had adopted in part the language, habits, religion, and morals of the whites. But slavery had not made them thrifty, self-reliant, or educated. Frederick Douglass said of the negro at the end of his servitude: "He had none of the conditions of self-preservation or self-protection. He was free from the individual master, but he had nothing but the dusty road under his feet. He was free from the old quarter that once gave him shelter, but a slave to the rains of summer and to the frosts of winter. He was turned loose, naked, hungry, and destitute to the open sky."

To prove that he was free the negro thought he must leave his old master, change his name, quit work for a time, perhaps get a new wife, and hang around the Federal soldiers in camp or garrison, or go to the towns where the Freedmen's Bureau was in process of organization. To the negroes who remained at home—and, curiously enough, for a time at least many did so—the news of freedom was made known somewhat ceremonially by the master or his representative. The negroes were summoned to the "big house," told that they were free, and advised to stay on for a share of the crop. The description by Mrs. Clayton, the wife of a Southern general, will serve for many: "My husband said, 'I think it best for me to inform our negroes of their freedom.' So he ordered all the grown slaves to come to him, and told them they no longer belonged to him as property, but were all free. 'You are not bound to remain with me any longer, and I have a proposition to make you. If any of you desire to leave, I propose to furnish you with a conveyance to move you and with provisions for the balance of the year.' The universal answer was, 'Master, we want to stay right here with you.' In many instances the slaves were so infatuated with the idea of being, as they said, 'free as birds' that they left their homes and consequently suffered; but our slaves were not so foolish."

The negroes, however, had learned of their freedom before their old masters returned from the war; they were aware that the issues of the war involved in some way the question of their freedom or servitude, and through the "grape vine telegraph," the news brought by the invading soldiers, and talk among the whites, they had long been kept fairly well informed. What the idea of freedom meant to the negroes it is difficult to say. Some thought that there would be no more work and that all would be cared for by the Government; others believed that education and opportunity were about to make them the equal of their masters. The majority of them were too bewildered to appreciate anything except the fact that they were free from enforced labor.

Former Slaves Speak Out

Two former slaves, Toby Jones and John McCoy, describe their lives after emancipation in the following excerpts.

Source: Botkin, ed. *Lay My Burden Down: A Folk History of Slavery* (University of Chicago Press, 1945).

Toby Jones

I worked for Massa 'bout four years after freedom, 'cause he forced me to, said he couldn't 'ford to let me go. His place was near ruint, the fences burnt, and the house would have been, but it was rock. ... When the war was over, Massa come home and says, "You son of a gun, you's supposed to be free, but you ain't, 'cause

53

I ain't gwine give you freedom." So I goes on working for him till I gits the chance to steal a hoss from him. The woman I wanted to marry, Govie, she 'cides to come to Texas with me. Me and Govie, we rides that hoss 'most a hundred miles, then we turned him a-loose and give him a scare back to his house, and come on foot the rest the way to Texas.

All we had to eat was what we could beg, and sometimes we went three days without a bite to eat. Sometimes we'd pick a few berries. When we got cold we'd crawl in a bushpile and hug up close together to keep warm. Once in a while we'd come to a farmhouse, and the man let us sleep on cottonseed in his barn, but they was far and few between, 'cause they wasn't many houses in the country them days like now.

When we gits to Texas, we gits married, but all they was to our wedding am we just 'grees to live together as man and wife. I settled on some land, and we cut some trees and split them open and stood them on end with the tops together for our house. Then we deadened some trees, and the land was ready to farm. There was some wild cattle and hogs, and that's the way we got our start, caught some of them and tamed them.

I don't know as I 'spected nothing from freedom, but they turned us out like a bunch of stray dogs, no homes, no clothing, no nothing, not 'nough food to last us one meal. After we settles on that place, I never seed man or woman, 'cept Govie, for six years, 'cause it was a long ways to anywhere. All we had to farm with was sharp sticks. We'd stick holes and plant corn, and when it come up we'd punch up the dirt around it. We didn't plant cotton, 'cause we couldn't eat that. I made bows and arrows to kill wild game with, and we never went to a store for nothing. We made our clothes out of animal skins.

John McCoy

Freedom wasn't no different I knows of. I works for Marse John just the same for a long time. He say one morning, "John, you can go out in the field iffen you wants to or you can get out iffen you wants to, 'cause the government say you is free. If you wants to work I'll feed you and give you clothes but can't pay you no money. I ain't got none." Humph, I didn't know nothing what money was, nohow, but I knows I'll git plenty victuals to eat, so I stays till Old Marse die and Old Miss git shut of the place. Then I gits me a job farming, and when I gits too old for that I does this and that for white folks, like fixing yards.

I's black and just a poor old nigger, but I reverence my white folks 'cause they reared me up in the right way. If colored folks pay 'tention and listen to what the white folks tell them, the world would be a heap better off. Us old niggers knows that's the truth, too, 'cause we larns respect and manners from our white folks, and on the great day of judgment my white folks is gwine to meet me and shake hands with me and be glad to see me. Yes, sir, that's the truth!

Negro Education

The Problem of Negro Education

The problem of how to educate thousands of illiterate freed slaves needed to be addressed. The federal government created the Freedmen's Bureau, whose one of many responsibilities was to set up school's and teach the freed slaves. Later, African American vocational schools like the Tuskeegee Institute and the Hampton Institute, and African American colleges like Howard University and Fisk University were established. In 1873, Helen W. Ludlow examined the problem of Negro education.

Source: Helen W. Ludlow, "The Hampton Normal and Agricultural Institute," *Harper's New Monthly Magazine,* XLVII, October, 1873. From *THE SOUTH: A Documentary History*, by Ina Woestemeyer Van Noppen (Princeton, New Jersey: D. Van Nostrand Company, Inc., 1958).

The ten years that separate us from the Proclamation of Emancipation have wrought some natural but curious changes in public sentiment, both North and South. ... One of the most important questions that the years have settled is that of negro education. The best thinkers of the North and South, however distant their stand-points, are no longer apart in the conclusion that it is of vital importance to the nation. This conviction is shown at the South by the action taken by most of the reconstructed States in embodying some provision for the negroes in their free-school system, and quite as remarkably by the increasing favor, or tolerance, to say the least, extended to the schools and colleges for freedmen established in them by Northern benevolence. ... It is a curious fact that the only institution south of the national capital which ... offers to destitute youth, an opportunity to earn at once a solid English education and a valuable industrial training, is a college for negroes. The Normal and Agricultural Institute of Hampton, Virginia, and its rapid growth and success, prove the adaptation of its system to the public needs.

Another demand of the South, which may be expected to continue and increase for some time, is that of colored teachers for its colored schools. ... The colored teacher ... is called upon not only to teach in the schoolhouses, but in the cabin; to advise the people how to build better houses, and raise better crops, and be better citizens. He is to be a little centre of civilization among them, and help, in his proper degree, to elevate his race by the power of his own life. His education should not unfit him to dwell among them; a poor man himself, he should be able at any time to enter the workshops or the fields, and make up the deficiencies of his often ill-paid salary. ...

Conditions in the Negro Schools

This selection is from a report written about the condition in "Negro" schools.

Source: *Atlantic Monthly,* Vol. 50, 1882. From *THE SOUTH: A Documentary History*, by Ina Woestemeyer Van Noppen (Princeton, New Jersey: D. Van Nostrand Company, Inc., 1958).

Many of the negro schools are maintained under great disadvantages and inconveniences. ... Here is an instance: I saw two colored men at work in one room with a school in which the average daily attendance for the winter was one hundred and twenty-six. They had to conduct recitations at the same time in opposite corners of the room. The house was open and very cold. The teachers were obliged to furnish fuel, and to provide desks, brooms, blackboards, and all other appliances at their own expense. The school was free to the pupils, the salaries of the teachers being paid for out of the public school fund. The house in which the school was maintained was owned by some Northern missionary or aid society, and was held by colored trustees, living in the town in which it was situated. They were too poor to repair or improve the building, and the (white) pubic school officers would not (perhaps could not under the law) appropriate anything for repairs to the house, unless the colored people would surrender their title to the property, which they declined to do. ...

Teachers often had to bring their own chairs to the make-shift schools.

It is very interesting to listen to the singing in the colored schools. I several times heard many hundred children singing together the old plantation and revival melodies, and other songs of their race. Some of these are very peculiar and wonderful. One hears everywhere a few rich and powerful voices, and the negro churches in the larger towns have fine choirs. But the old negro music will soon disappear. All the educated negro ministers discourage or forbid the use of it among their people, and the strange, wild songs, whether religious or not, are coming to be regarded as relics and badges of the old condition of slavery and heathenism, and the young men and women are ashamed to sing them.

Booker T. Washington

Booker T. Washington was an educator and spokesman for African Americans, encouraging them to get an education and become economically independent. He thought a vocational education was the best way to prepare African Americans for better economic opportunities. Washington himself received a vocational education at the Hampton Institute in Virginia. He later founded and built the Tuskeegee Institute in Alabama, to provide Blacks with an institution in which to acquire vocational education and job training.

Source: Booker T. Washington, *Up From Slavery: An Autobiography* (Garden City, New York: Doubleday, 1963).

The years from 1867 to 1878 I think may be called the period of Reconstruction. This included the time that I spent as a student at Hampton and as a teacher in West Virginia. During the whole of the Reconstruction period two ideas were constantly agitating the minds of the coloured people, or, at least, the minds of a large part of the race. One of these was the craze for Greek and Latin learning, and the other was a desire to hold office.

It could not have been expected that a people who had spent generations in slavery, and before that generations in the darkest heathenism, could at first form any proper conception of what an education meant. In every part of the South, during the Reconstruction period, schools, both day and night, were filled to overflowing with people of all ages and conditions, some being as far along in age as sixty and seventy years. The ambition to secure an education was most praiseworthy and encouraging. The idea, however, was too prevalent that, as soon as one secured a little education, in some unexplainable way he would be free from most of the hardships of the world, and, at any rate, could live without manual labour. There was a further feeling that a knowledge however little, of the Greek and Latin languages would make one a very superior human being, something bordering almost on the supernatural. I remember that the first coloured man whom I saw who knew something about foreign languages impressed me at that time as being a man of all others to be envied.

Naturally, most of our people who received some little education became teachers or preachers. While among these two classes there were many capable, earnest, godly men and women, still a large proportion took up teaching or preaching as an easy way to make a living. Many became teachers who could do little more than write their names. I remember there came into our neighborhood one of this class, who was in search of a school to teach, and the question arose while he was there as to the shape of the earth and how he would teach the children concerning this subject. He explained his position in the matter by saying that he was prepared to teach that the earth was either flat or round, according to the preference of a majority of his patrons.

....

During the whole of the Reconstruction period our people throughout the South looked to the Federal Government for everything, very much as a child looks to its mother. This was not unnatural. The central government gave them freedom, and the whole Nation had been enriched for more than two centuries by the labour of the Negro. Even as a youth, and later in manhood, I had the feeling that it was cruelly wrong in the central government, at the beginning of our freedom, to fail to make some provision for the general education of our people in addition to what the states might do, so that the people would be better prepared for the duties of citizenship.

During the time I was a student in Washington the city was crowded with coloured people, many of whom had recently come from the South. A large proportion of these people had been drawn to Washington because they felt that they could lead a life of ease there. Others had secured minor government positions, and still another large class was there in the hope of securing Federal positions. A number of coloured men—some of them very strong and brilliant—were in the House of Representatives at that time, and one, the Hon. B. K. Bruce, was in the Senate. All this tended to make Washington an attractive place for members of the coloured race. Then, too, they knew that at all times they could have the protection of the law in the District of Columbia. The public schools in Washington for coloured people were better then than they were elsewhere. I took great interest in studying the life of our people there closely at that time. I found that while among them there was a large element of substantial, worthy citizens, there was also a superficiality about the life of a large class that greatly alarmed me. I saw young coloured men who were not earning more than four dollars a week spend two dollars or more for a buggy on Sunday to ride up and down Pennsylvania Avenue in order that they might try to convince the world that they were worth thousands. I saw other young men who received seventy-five or one hundred dollars per month from the Government, who were in debt at the end of every month. I saw men who but a few months previous were members of Congress, then without employment and in poverty. Among a large class there seemed to be a dependence upon the Government of every conceivable thing. ...

In Washington I saw girls whose mothers were earning their living by laundering. These girls were taught by their mothers, in rather a crude way it is true, the industry of laundrying. Later these girls entered the public schools and remained there perhaps six or eight years. When the public-school course was finally finished, they wanted more costly dresses, more costly hats and shoes. In a word, while their wants had been increased, their ability to supply their wants had not been increased in the same degree. On the other hand, their six or eight years of book education had weaned them away from the occupation of their mothers. The result of this was too many cases that the girls went to the bad. I often thought how much wiser it would have been to give these girls the same amount of mental training—and I favour any kind of training, whether in the languages or mathematics, that gives strength and culture to the mind—but at the same time to give them the most thorough training in the latest and best methods of laundrying and other kindred occupations.

The Black Vote

In 1870, the Fifteenth Amendment became law. African American males had finally won the right to vote, but problems arose in the southern states over this law. Many felt that African Americans should not have been given the vote so soon after emancipation. Critics believed that since most African Americans were illiterate, they could not understand politics. There were also lingering tensions between ex-Confederates who were stripped of their voting rights, and the new voters.

Myrta Lockett describes dishonest voting practices that took place in the South in the following selections.

Source: Myrta Lockett, *Dixie After the War* (Boston: Houghton Mifflin Company, 1937).

The Southern ballot-box was the new toy of the Ward of the Nation; the vexation of housekeepers and farmers, the despair of statesmen, patriots, and honest men generally. Elections were preceded by political meetings, often incendiary in character, which all one's servants must attend. With election day, every voting precinct became a picnic-ground, to say no worse. Negroes went to precincts overnight and camped out. Morning revealed reinforcements arriving. All sexes and ages came afoot, in carts, in wagons, as to a fair or circus. Old women set up tables and spread out ginger-cakes and set forth buckets of lemonade. One famous campaign manager had all-night picnics in the woods, with bonfires, barrels of liquor, darkeys sitting around drinking, fiddling, playing the banjo, dancing. The instant polls opened they were marched up and voted.

Negroes almost always voted in companies. A leader, standing on a box, handed out tickets as they filed past. All were warned at Loyal Leagues to vote no ticket other than that given by the leader, usually a local preacher who could no more read the ballots he distributed than could the recipients. ...

Negroes were carried by droves from one county to another, one State to another, and voted over and over wherever white plurality was feared. Other tricks were to change polling-places suddenly, informing the negroes and not the whites; to scratch names from registration lists and substitute others. Whites would walk miles to a registration place to find it closed; negroes, privately advised, would have registered and gone. ...

The most lasting wrong reconstruction inflicted upon the South was in the inevitable political demoralisation of the white man. No one could regard the ballot-box as the voice of the people, as a sacred thing. It was a plaything, a jack-in-the-box for the darkeys, a conjurer's trick that brought drinks, tips and picnics. It was the carpet-bagger's stepping-stone to power. The votes of a multitude were for sale. ...

According to election law, when ballots polled exceeded registration lists, a blindfolded elector would put his hand in the box and withdraw until ballots and lists tallied. Many tissue ballots could be folded into one and voted as a single ballot; a little judicious agitation after they were in the box would shake them apart. ... Democrats and Republicans had each a manager. The Republican ran his hand into the box and gave it a stir; straightway it became so full it couldn't be shut, ballots falling apart and multiplying themselves. The Republicans laughed: "I have heard of self-raising flour. These are self-raising ballots." ...

64

The Lasting Impact of Reconstruction

Segregation Made Legal

by
Cheryl Edwards

Reconstruction policies and federal laws attempted to help
the South achieve racial equality. Many White southerners were
not ready to do this. They still promoted the idea that African
Americans were incapable of academic achievement and moral
behavior. They wanted all public places like schools, bathrooms,
hospitals, and beaches to become separate for each race. Signs
that read "whites only" and "blacks only" began to appear in
front of public facilities in southern towns and cities in the
1880s. White supremists and Southern lawmakers were creating
a segregated southern society. The Supreme Court also began
to challenge the civil rights of African Americans.

As early as 1876, the segregationists began to win their
war in the Supreme Court. In the case of the United States vs.
Cruikshank, the Supreme Court ruled that the federal government
could not protect the African Americans' rights of citizenship and
suffrage, which had been guaranteed under the Fourteenth and Fifteenth Amendments. In 1883, the Supreme Court eroded the civil
rights of African Americans even further. The Court ruled that
the Civil Rights Act of 1875, which guaranteed that people of all
races could use all public facilities, was unconstitutional.

By the 1880s, southern states had begun to pass the so-called
"Jim Crow" laws, which required African Americans to use separate public facilities. In 1896, the Supreme Court's decision in
the landmark Plessy vs. Fergusson case gave legal support to
segregation. The Court established the famous "separate but
equal" doctrine. The doctrine meant that states could segregate

65

their public facilities, as long as they provided the same type of facility for both African Americans and European Americans.

These legal decisions struck a crushing blow to African Americans. The Supreme Court's legal sanction of segregation permitted the southern states to deny African Americans the right to vote, to hold public office, to sit on a jury, to testify in court against a white man, and to use public facilities designated for "whites only".

To escape the unfair Jim Crow laws, many African Americans migrated to northern and western states. Others who chose to stay in the South established African American communities where they helped each other build businesses, schools and churches. African American leaders like Booker T. Washington and W.E.B. DuBois protested the segregation laws and the discriminatory practices against African Americans.

In 1898, race riots broke out in the cities of Memphis and New Orleans. The Ku Klux Klan continued to spread its form of hatred and violence. Lynchings became a popular means of intimidation against African Americans. The riots, the lynchings, the KKK activities, and the Jim Crow laws were aimed at isolating African Americans politically and psychologically. The forces that were stripping African Americans of their civil rights were once again trying to create a subservient and powerless place for them in southern society. For African Americans, the South became a hostile place in which to live. Segregation and racism became entrenched in southern politics and culture. Even today, one hundred years later, Americans still battle racism and prejudice in the on-going struggle for civil rights, a struggle not limited to the South.

Suggested Further Reading

Burns, Olive A., *A Cold Sassy Tree.* New York: Delta, 1992.

Current, Richard N., ed., *Those Terrible Carpetbaggers.* New York: Oxford University Press, 1988.

Faulkner, William, *The Unvanquished.* New York: Random House, 1938.

Hays, Jr., Ottis, "Reconstruction and the Five Civilized Tribes," *Cobblestone.* Peterborough, NH: May 1987.

McCarthy, Agnes, and Lawrence Reddick, *Worth Fighting For.* Garden City: Zenith Books, Doubleday & Co., 1965.

Mitchell, Margaret, *Gone With the Wind.* Boston: GK Hall, 1992.

Stampp, Kenneth M., *The Era of Reconstruction.* New York: Alfred A. Knopf, 1965.

Trelease, Allen W., *Reconstruction: The Great Experiment.* New York: Harper & Row, Publishers, Inc., 1971.

Welsh, Douglas, *The Civil War.* London: Bison Books Limited, 1982.

Yates, Elizabeth, *Amos Fortune: Free Man.* New York: Puffin Books, 1989.

About the Editor

Cheryl Edwards has degrees in history and anthropology from Michigan State University. She and her husband Jon spent two years doing archival research in London, Rome, Paris, and Brussells for Jon's doctoral thesis on Ethiopian history. While working in London's Public Records Office, Cheryl indexed 550 volumes of court records kept by the British in Addis Ababa, Ethiopia. "I have always enjoyed reading old documents and trying to figure out what shaped people's thoughts and actions. Historians are very much like detectives. It is their job to find primary sources, and interpret them."

As a teacher, Cheryl taught history and writing to students in Ohio, Michigan, and New Hampshire. Cheryl has been a freelance writer since 1985. She recently edited *Westward Expansion: Exploration and Settlement* in this Perspectives on History Series.